Grand Rising

A New Day Has Dawned

Messages, Music and Poetry

Grand Rising

A New Day Has Dawned

Copyright © 2024 by Cheryl Lunar Wind

Cheryl's poetry in this collection may be shared, printed with credit given to the author. All other contributors keep rights to their work.

Any Inquiries contact:

cheryl.hiller@yahoo.com

Some of the poems in this collection first appeared in

We Are One, Follow the White Rabbit, Know Your Way,

Come to Mount Shasta chapbooks; and on facebook.

Front cover photo taken by Cheryl Lunar Wind

Back cover credit goes to Christinemarie Spiritualdoorways

First edition.

Published by Alexander Agency Books, Mount Shasta, California 96067

ISBN 979-8-9897287-1-8

Preface

Grand Rising deals with the new energies of Gaia; her movement through the active Sun cycle and into the proton belt taking us into the age of Aquarius.

We are navigating, moving into the new; no longer surviving but now being able to thrive.

This book of messages helps readers to deal with integration of their past experiences and the rapidly changing state of upgradement we are experiencing.

This volume contains wise words of many light leaders. Much gratitude for all the sharing.

orenda- a mystical force present in all people that empowers them to affect the world, or to effect change in their own lives.

"So think about this:
How would you live your life
if you knew your prayers
were going to be answered?

Because that's exactly
how your prayers
are going to be answered.

That's the moment your life
becomes your prayer--
and the moment your prayer
becomes your life."
---Joe Dispenza, PhD

Contents

Dawn Upon The Mountain 1
by Bob Dunham

At Dawn by Maria Lodes 2

Ode to the 5th Dimension by Cheryl 3

The Visit(Lemurians) by Darrel Johannes 4,5

My Soul Remains by Cody Ray Richardson 6

Soul by Cheryl 7

The Firewalker Wears His Scars 8
by Cody Ray Richardson

Marbles by Omanassa Star 9

The Long Walk by Mercy Talley 10

Loosen Your Grip by Susan Grace 11

Trippy Times by Mary Long 12,13

Sometimes by Marcie Bakker 14

Memories by Gracia Penttinen 15

What is your holographic climate? 16
by Le'Vell Zimmerman

How Do You Feel? 17
by Susan Grace

Go On Out 18
by Cody Ray Richardson

Gift of Process 19
by Le'Vell Zimmerman

Keep Both As Friends 20
by Cody Ray Richardson

Acceptance by Le'Vell Zimmerman 21

Smile by Cody Ray Richardson 22

De-Construct by anonymous 23

Life Is But a Dream 24
by Le'Vell Zimmerman

Partner-Ship by Cheryl 24

Answer the Phone 25
by Cheryl

Salvation 26
by Mitchell T. Miller and Alyssa Narum

Always by Emily River 27

Short Quotes 28

Change Is Hard by Susan Grace 29

To Mother Wind by Eden Sky 30,31

Falling Skies by Bob Dunham 32

Third Dollar by Bob Dunham 32

Look Forward to The Dawn 33
by Bob Dunham

Love's Truth 34
by Mercy Talley

This Now Moment by Cheryl 35

Grand Rising by Cheryl 36
quote by
Christinemarie Spiritualdoorways

the event by Cheryl 37

In the 5th Dimension 38
by Shianna Freeman

Love Unconditional 39
by Jennifer H.

Gentle 40, 41
by Cody Ray Richardson

Just Be 42
by Cheryl

Mastery 43
by Le'Vell Zimmerman

Contributors page

Author page &
Testimonials

Dawn Upon The Mountain
by Bob Dunham

Crystal clouds cannot conceal
that which we know
and feel is real

Hovering hanging however low
like all they'll pass
the wind will blow

Gusty gales grabbing trees
clear the air
and then we see

Forgotten forests forming again
At Dawn
Up on the Mountain

At Dawn
by Maria Lodes

Returning to Wholeness
    —early morning
Eyes open
     —focus Within

Seeing the world
    through an Inner Eye—
Door opens wide
    —glorious the View

Quiet and peaceful
     —filled with Love
A taste of Reality
     —Who I Am

World transforms
     —wondrous to me
Me who has shrunk back
     —a witness at most

A place of Knowing
     —impermanence
Wanting to stay
     —where wanting is taboo

A demanding world
    pulls me back—
It comes with amnesia
     —forgot who I Am

The vision a Gift
     —will return again
Cleansing old habits
    rigid ways of the mind...

Left behind
    a glimpse of sun Light
Glancing off dawn's
    precious dewdrops...

Ode to the 5th Dimension
by Cheryl

Time Jump
      to your right place!
Join the Age of Aquarius.
Let the Sun shine in.
"I'm not the only one staring at the Sun."

Rub your crystals
Thank the trees,
ancient spirits they are.

Today is Sun Day,
Day of the Sun.
Day of gathering
at the park---

Drumming, Strumming, Dancing.

Feeling Free
Wiping the slate
Forgiving the past.

Memories of past loves
Pop Up
to be acknowledged.

We can dance
on both sides of the coin---
Multi-task
Multi-dimensional beings are we
Not just this crude form.

I Shine
my dance of light
for all to see.

Translucent---
Clear in my intentions
Recognition in our eyes
Speaking
the Universal thought.

The Visit (Lemurians)
by Darrel Johannes

Many of us were gathered on a farm in a hilly and green countryside. All about various tasks and leisures.
The sky was clear,
temperature perfect, some light clouds in blue sky.
I felt a stir, something strange but secure, an odd sense of wonder was palatable. Many folks started looking outward and upward, some kind of front runner preceded an energy, an orb of sorts moving towards our gathering.
The orbs then manifested into some kind of flying creatures that had people on them. They looked middle aged and healthy. There were legions of them across the sky. I had no fear just wonder. It seemed as if they were asking questions, scouting, collecting information or samples of some kind.

They didn't say much, they certainly seemed not happy to be here. Dutiful and committed, but pleased about their mission no. Everyone saw them, not one person at the gathering denied their existence, one could not deny what was so blazingly real before their eyes.

I found myself wanting to get my face as close to their faces as I could. I trusted them, as no being I have ever trusted before. They were sound, wise, good willed and incredibly intelligent. It was as if they knew the future as well as the past. They had been around, for sure but were not hardened or discouraged by what they had experienced. All of their understanding was key to right action. They knew exactly what to do, when to do it and how to do it. I had the feeling that everything on this planet is going to work out for the good of all.

They had different complexions, male and female, different personalities and dispositions.
But all had the same resolve, compassion and duty.
There was this hillbilly type couple hanging out by the fire; they were young and seemed a bit new at the job. I was very comfortable with them. The guy was sleeping, or at least trying to, on the hard ground, with just a blanket and pillow. The gal was warming by the fire. She said I know he loves me, wants to marry me; I can just tell by the way he speaks to me.

They were so precious, It would make you cry.

It was all so very natural, the way they were.
They seemed human but more,
a much higher quality of human than we are.
They were clear and straight and such very very good souls.
It was as if they had been us at one time, been there, done that,
and not going back. No desire to go back, no desire
to give up heaven for hell.

They didn't smile much, and actually showed very little
passion as we know it. They didn't need to. Their visit,
their mission here was passion enough. Their level of
concern and commitment to us and our greatest good
said it all. A smile would have been just fluff.

Each persons reaction to these beings was one on one.
Their reaction was no way a group or mob response.
Each person related to them on the level they were,
and ready and willing to accept. Each reaction
would determine the individual experience
and how far they could go.
There was no pressure to be a certain way, a
complete exercise of free will.
The offer was there, what
you did with it, was up to you!

These beings were disaffected by our world, frankly,
seemed unimpressed. They had disdain for the cultural norms,
economic systems and our treatment of the planet and each other.
They seemed to be aware of what would happen to them if they
adapted to this place.

I don't think they can spend much time here without going back to
regroup and plan the next move. They left just as they came, on
creatures that took them back up and then into pure white energy.

There is no way to control them, NONE. They know the game
and refuse to play. I feel like I just made the best friends
anyone could ever have. I trust you, I love you.
Please, Please come back.

My Soul Remains
by Cody Ray Richardson

Two personalities fighting inside my head.
One wants me to succeed the other wants me dead.
An old self a new self a higher self a low self.
One that comes from scarcity another from wealth.
One pretending and defending idealizations it can never uphold.
Another trusting in faith as the Great mystery unfolds.
All the organisms inside me that they draw in to feed.
Some of them positive some of them full of negativity.
When will these two personalities merge? Which one of them will win?
Which one of them will die first? Or do I need both of them to survive?
Does everyone experience this that is alive?
Did something walk into me when my body had died?
A higher better self to help me survive?
All of these questions go unanswered and rot me from the inside.
The sands inside my hourglass rip at me like sand being washed away from the tide.
Does it really matter if the glass around me shatters?
Was it just the thing or the protective shell,
Who really inside me can never be destroyed.
Oh, what a story that is yet for me to tell.
I try to explain what I've seen on the other side of the Veil.
It's so confusing for everyone, oh well.
I'll get back in line and put on my happy face.
Inside is my two personalities who fight over my mortal body,
still my soul remains an eternal well.

Soul
by Cheryl

See that little black spot by the sun today?

It's my soul out there,
Searching for a way home.

I am a dove---cast out
of Noah's Ark.

Hunting
for a branch of my own.

Jumbled feelings and memories
glide by--
briefly--
not long enough--
to get--
a foothold.

Same old thing as yesterday.

The impermanence of it all.

My mind is a sentry--
guards against,
lies, traps, and endless detours.

My soul longs for home.

The Firewalker Wears His Scars
by Cody Ray

Can't stitch the heart
Time expands the tears
Tears become rivers in the sand of memories
Perfect haunting images
A reality that was never real
Expectations of the past yet to be fulfilled
Should have and could haves laugh
Long gone is the person
Bigger is the hurt
Why know now what could not be seen then
Now the boat has sailed
On the shore of oblivion
I held my breath while drowning in tears
Lonely from if onlys
Piled in the subconscious
Regret is my ill best friend
Why them and no one else
Why can I not decree love
The one thing that matters unreachable
Is it only a fantasy of the mad
Unfulfilling self prophecy
Over and over until deep under
Sewn in a place unmovable
A sword in a broken heart
Never to be pulled from it's place
A piece of glass deep in my foot
The only thing that remains
A reminder of a failure
The Firewalker Wears His Scars

Marbles
by Omanassa Star

Have you lost your marbles?
It was one of those expressions I grew up with;
and was used when we were acting up, or a little crazy.

Yet, when I was a little girl, I didn't know that is what
it meant.

So, when my very angry Dad had asked my big brother
if he'd "lost his marbles" I was listening. When my
brother got very upset because of the lost marbles,
I decided to help out and brought him some of mine
to make him feel good.

I didn't at all understand, why he threw them away,
and didn't even thank me.----

The Long Walk
by Mercy Talley

It's been such a long
obstacle strewn walk,
for lifetimes,
at times I'm exhausted
to the core of my Being & Soul...
where All that Matters
Is that Loving Light
Prevails
& cruel usurpers every tactic fails
dissolving as dust on
distant planets..
So finally Huemyn Kind
Will flourish ~ thriving
In the Beauty & Creativity
Of Love's Truth & Peace ~

...whether I make it this time
Or The Next...

Loosen Your Grip
by Susan Grace

Holding on to the story of how you got here,
Can sometimes be a habituated response to
Heading into the unknown.

You learn from your lived experience, for sure.
When you hold on to the story too tightly,
You stop creating.

You loose your empowerment.

It's past time to loosen your grip on the story.

*Where you're headed is far beyond what you've
seen so far.*

The more you migrate from--
The obsolete past into the rapidly evolving present,
The more secure you'll feel going forward.

You are way more adaptable than you realize.
You'll see.

Trippy Times
by Mary Long

These energies are downright weird.

Some days nothing makes sense, other days old dense feelings come up.
Then there is this space of emptiness, where nothing matters,
I just sit here looking out the window for hours and get lost in it.
Sometimes I even lose how long I have been in this zone of empty space.
Is this part of our Ascension?

Are we emptying ourselves completely and finally moving into our full 5th Dimensional Consciousness?
We aren't there yet, because until we do--
we cannot take all this old energy with us into the new,
we just have to keep working on ourselves until we have fully let go of it all and become completely empty.

It isn't easy navigating our way through life right now because everything just feels different.

Our consciousness is nudging at us to create something new,
but we just aren't quite sure where to go, how to do it, even though we do.
If that makes sense.
I am telling you all these energies are trippy and making me spacey.
Can't stay focused on something for too long because if I do, I feel dazed and confused.
My brain doesn't want to think, it just wants to flow, flow with whatever comes.

I know during the summer we are supposed to be getting some pretty awesome downloads (where we feel all lovey and fuzzy inside).
I feel that now, and it is like I am straddling worlds.
Either that or we are being prepared for them coming, all I can say is I just feel downright weird.
Like I am constantly walking in a dream world, but when I am sleeping, I am everywhere, seem to be traveling many different timelines or dimensions.

I just feel weird when I have my eyes open trying to function in this 3d World we are still experiencing.
I don't know how else to explain it, I feel this is all part of it.

God knows if I have to use my brain, if it will work. LOL.
I am really having a hard time explaining my experiences.
I look out the window and I feel everything out there, even the trees.
Birds come up to the limb by the window and stare into me,
like they are connecting with my Soul.
Anyone else feeling this, or is it just me?
I suppose when you are just in the flow of it all
you are going to have some trippy experiences.
I know my frequency is high---
I have so far blown out my cook stove, my phone isn't working right, and I think I blew the electrical outlet where my microwave was.
Maybe I should wrap myself up in some copper wire, so I don't short things out, lol.
Even before I pump gas into the car, I touch the metal on my car to make sure my fingers aren't going to spark.

Just staying in the moment, letting it all happen and see how it all comes out.
Trippy times and I can't even read anything from the powers that were, because absolutely nothing they do makes sense.
Riding it out Loves.
Hopefully these Sparks I am emitting from this body will spark my Spirit to just keep going higher.
You know me, some days I just ramble, this is one of them.

Sometimes
by Marcie Bakker

Sometimes,
I slip into timelessness,
At play with my friends,
Or worshiping the Sun,
Stop, breathe, look at the stars.

Sometimes,
As a child, I would cry,
I felt 'I want to go home',
Sick with homesickness,
Regardless of my location.

Sometimes,
At my grandparent's house,
I felt like I was in the past,
While being in the present,
I knew I was living a memory.

Sometimes,
Now I visit my parents and theirs,
My imagination is a reality,
Encouragement for the density,
The archer is aiming her bow.

Memories (Piece by Piece)
by Gracia Penttinen

Among my memories I found a description of myself
that I wrote 14 years ago. The challenge was to write
a story that starts with the letter P.
Still find this funny...

Small snippets from my path,
Piece by Piece
With P popping in the drawing:
Peed a lot while being a cheerful bawler.
Bouncing like a little girl, a bottle standing on top of puffs.
Little boys and girls in the playground.

Neutral, impartial, cracking up on the nut-crazy
decisions of politicians.

Cracking frost, excited speakers blow.
On dry days, basking on the surface,
to worship sunrise and sunset.
Slowly barking, long-minded
treading the path of the shepherd.
Long, red-cheeked, revealer of holy places.

A painted semi-traveler in its place,
a tormented worshiper of the pyramids.
Puritan who left Panohommi.

Currently cheerfully picking thorns
from the little dog's buttocks.
Pumpkin soft kisses for cheerful hiking buddies
in the mail.

What is your holographic climate?
by Le'Vell Zimmerman

The nature of your reality is often fueled by the suggestions and experiences of yourself and others that you have accepted within.

Once again, you get to decide to accept these ideas or not as a Source energy being.

For example; a soul will say, "Men are like this, and Women do that...", where none of this has to be true for you unless you continue to accept these programs or configurations within your reality.

Just know that it is truly a choice what "holographic climate" you live in beloved, where even your defense from these experiences is a form of energetic investment, crystallizing the evidence of such programs.

What's true for others doesn't have to be true for you within this hologram, where all are living in their own unique environment based on their own frequency of being.

This is an infinite universe of infinite possibilities, where you get to decide the timeline and configuration you are experiencing as a soul.

Love or Fear.
The choice is yours.

#3333

How Do You Feel?
by Susan Grace

Any brave calls you're making
That will have a long term impact
Need to involve you being honest about
how you feel.

No matter how much sense you make of
what's in front of you,
If you try to bypass your human emotions,
Your intentions won't land right.

Fear, apprehension, overwhelm;
Vulnerable, exposed, raw;
Hopeful, open, wanting--

How do you really, truly feel?
At least be honest with yourself.
You don't want unaddressed emotions
sneaking up on you later.

Go On Out
by Cody Ray Richardson

Put those books back on the shelf.
Get out of the house.
Take yourself out.
Those lips won't kiss themselves.
What is he without you?
He can't solve your puzzle without a clue.
Only you can be his secret ingredient.
You have to send to be heaven sent.
So forget about your past regret.
For you, for him and for him your meant.

Gift of Process
by Le'Vell Zimmerman

You have stated your intentions here already beloved.

Allow life to answer you...

Relax.

Know that all is happening like this on purpose.

You are being shown what you need to experience now for the next part of the journey.

Linear time provides you with the gift of "process".

Being sophisticated enough to know that "the story" is the prize as well is reflective of your capacity of spiritual maturity beloved.

Masters know this.

"Don't miss your own movies beloved"...

#333

Keep Both as Friends
by Cody Ray Richardson

Who am I to say who they are?
The divine orchestra orchestrates
Some I hold, some I push away
The lessons they carry prevail
The reason we meet unknown
All diamonds in the rough
Mystery unfolding
Will I learn the lesson with this one?
Will another deliver the message?
All the same, yet in different languages
Let go
Learn or be ripped apart hanging on
Can I kill my ego to save my soul--
Maybe this time I will keep both as friends
A tea party with all the archetypes
A song with all the parts of the divine
Or a limited playlist of my choosing?

Acceptance
by Le'Vell Zimmerman

Beyond being "right or wrong", it's important to acknowledge reflections and be acknowledged emotionally beloved.

The depth of your compassion is beyond logical analysis, where harmonious coexistence and collaboration is necessary for any relationship to be sustainable.

It's unwise to attempt to force anything.

You can trust that whatever is supposed to happen will do so naturally.

It requires great capacity of strength to accept.

#333

Smile
by Cody Ray Richardson

A memory covering a memory.
An experience over an experience.
Like stacking rocks on one another.
Does this really change anything?
How do we feng shui our mind?
The records remain somatically.
The triggers waiting to bring them up.
To be lived over and over.
The murders celebrate the one child kept.
I celebrate death dats more than birth.
Finally there, free.
Free from a pile that can't be cleaned.
Free from the illusion that life is fine.
A wise man in the mountain.
A beggar on the hill.
They suffer the same.
No matter how they are seen.
No matter how they see themselves.
We are meant to love each other.
The problem is we need another to do so.
So superficial are the brief relationships.
So rare is lasting love.
Only to held through the night.
To meet her singing in the bath.
I both dread and am thankful for the time.
Time spent feeling love.
Time spent not feeling love.
One day the pile will burn.
On that day I will smile.
For I know my days of love have passed.
I can only cheer on those who've made it.
The family people.
I watch and cheer for them.
So lucky God smiled on them.
So thankful some are chosen.
I smile for them.
Maybe next life they will smile for me.

De-Construct
by anonymous

Sips of air
Gulps of blood
Satisfaction till noon

Glimpse of death
Molts of mud
Sepal until bloom

Tread the waters carefully
Its meaning often misconstrued
taking apart deliberately
the self yourself imbued

Life Is But a Dream
by Le'Vell Zimmerman

It's all planned out this way.

The more you are able to remain
centered emotionally,
the more graceful
your journey will be.

Gently down the stream...

#4343

Partner--Ship
by Cheryl

Journey in Peace.
Just Go.
No matter how Long & Winding
the Road--
allow the journey.

Whether Stagecoach, Spaceship
or Boat--
Journey in peace--

Be a good neighbor, passenger,
traveler--

Partner--Ship.

"It's not the destination, but the journey."

Answer the Phone
by Cheryl

Waves of words
turn into waterfalls,
Storming
in my ears
Ringing
like an insistent caller

Repeating numbers
Until I answer--

Bellowing, behind doors
Only I can hear.

Salvation
By Mitchell Miller and Alyssa Narum

Everybody here has a part within Creation
Everybody here has a heart with motivation

So which way will you go?
And will you choose to grow
To higher realization
For the choice is yours
To open up the doors
To live within, Salvation

Worry not my fellow friend
For it is already yours
All the Light and Love you share
It is the greatest cure
So stand strong
As you move on
For it is already yours
Worry not my fellow friend
For it is already yours

Salvation

Everybody here has a gift to discover
Everybody here can uplift one another

So which way will you go?
And will you choose to grow
To higher realization
For the choice is yours
To open up the doors
To live within, Salvation

Worry not my fellow friend
For it is already yours
All the Light and Love you share
It is the greatest cure
So stand strong
As you move on
For it is already yours
Worry not my fellow friend
For it is already yours, Salvation

Always beside
by Emily River

Life is a trip--
Enjoy the journey

Be a good human
Spread the right vibe

Always--
Eye will always do right
with and for myself,
no one above
no one below
always beside.

Short Quotes

Oasis by Cody

Acceptance is the magic rejuvenating Oasis
within the desert of self punishment.

Mathin' by Susan

It's all been worth it.
You would not undo the lesson.

Come on now.
The math is about to start mathin'.

Pain by Varunvir

Denial of Pain is Suffering.
Pain itself is not.
Infact Understanding Pain is Awakening.

Emotional Ransom by Cheryl

I'll do this
if you do that--

Void by A'Marie

"Endlessly searching and seeking
Yet never fully understanding
The knowledge fails to fill
The void within..."

There is a void within that can only be filled within.

Intelligence by Le'Vell

"There is great intelligence
in the space of innocent observation and acceptance."

Change Is Hard
by Susan Grace

You absolutely can double down on
Trying to force what you're used to
Being your safe place going forward.

It won't work, but you can try.

Anything that will not stand the test of time
Has been dismantling for years.
It's costing you too much energy to force the old to work.

But change is hard;
The unknown is overwhelming to human vulnerability;
and the ego's need for control is stubborn.

However, you're existing within completely different energy now.
It's future forward and frequency-based.
It's about alignment, not rigid insistence devoid of deviation.

If you're going to double down on anything--
appeal to your ego the need for self agency--
Consider letting it be on your dedication to evolving
without unnecessary resistance.

~ To Mother Wind ~ by Eden Sky

Whirler of Worlds
Queen of Her own Heart
She rules the realm
Empress of the Ethereal
Skydancer
She divines the Time
Unconquerable
as
She
moves
in moods
and speaks
in tempos
curls and coaxes
hints and flirts
swirls and merges
pushes, weaves
screams and screeches
hums
knocks, howls, rocks
calms and cleanses
bellows, brushes
whispers, rushes
reaches, murmurs
humbles
yes
She
teaches
a heavenly caress
She can be
a holy blanket
woven of warm
mystery
She can soothe
seduce
shake
ravage
shift
uplift
dissolve
destroy
She seeks

to shock us
free
from
staleness
to breathe
instead
Her living
joy
Uncontainable
She dispels boundaries
Wise Mother
Keeper of Currents
Her stillness is
pure poise
punctuating
the passionate precision
She configures her curves, arcs
trails of transcendental rivers
through air,
knocking over human thoughts
with the vitality of vastness
raw as only It is
alive as only this shapeshifting touch
of Her flux
of perpetual nowness
offering this fleeting taste to our senses
She breaks open the moment
and frees it beyond itself
Mother of living salvation
chariot of light in motion
She calls us to meet
the centerless core of Her
moving mandala
that no memory can touch
but that we can ride
if only we open
our wings
to soar
upon the untameable
pulse
of our own
sovereign
spirit's
wind

Falling Skies
by Bob Dunham

It's raining fire on me all around.
The reigning hierarchy is gaining ground.
Your barnyard riddles at first so sly.
Replaced the egg and chicken with the maggot and fly.
Children sing dirges old gasoline cars.
Their parents are buying a ticket to Mars.
Or selling you one, if you're in the market.

Third Dollar
by Bob Dunham

You come out of your haze
You've been sleeping for days
And one thing seems to keep coming back
Asleep or Awake
We give and we take
Bright nights and days dark black

They come and they go
The change is slow
But speed doesn't matter
Just know it's there
In the future
Somewhere
Gives the Hope
It Will Be Better

Look Forward to The Dawn
music by Bob Dunham

Don't worry about days in your past you regret
And don't worry about days that aren't even here yet
We've got to live today before it slips right away
Everything will work out some way

No don't forget the past it has many truths to teach
And don't forget your hopes for the future
Though tomorrow's just out of reach
Let go of the guilt you've carried so long (of days forever gone)
Let go of the fears you've carried for years
And Look Forward to The Dawn, Look Forward to The Dawn

Don't worry if thoughts of days gone by bring a tear
And don't worry if tomorrow stirs feelings of fear
We've got to live right now or we might forget how
Everything will work out somehow

No don't forget the past it has many truths to teach
And don't forget your hopes for the future
Though tomorrow's just out of our reach
Let go of the guilt you've carried so long (of days forever gone)
Let go of the fears you've carried for years
And Look Forward to The Dawn, Look Forward to The Dawn

Love's Truth
by Mercy Talley

True Restoration Occurs
When We Deeply Release
old concepts &
mental constructs
that can not support
new foundations
of fresh perspectives
aligned with Truth
~
Releasing
Back to
Origin of
True Source
Is What
Forgiveness
Is
~
May My / Our
Hunger be fulfilled
With the Manna
of Love's Truth
~
It is Time
To Command
Into Being
The Truth
Be Known
By All

This Now Moment
by Cheryl

down
the long and winding road---
I hear singing--
--ancient songs--

The old ones are returning--
there is a sacred noise,
--Ringing of the bell.
Waking me up
early, like an alarm clock.

White Buffalo Calf Woman---
stands for rebirth, renewal
of the sacred ways---

Remembrance.

The Knowing---
you can have it.
Keep it---
It is a gift.

We all have many gifts.
Do we share---
Wear them proudly--
Or hide them?

Jesus said--
Don't hide your light under a basket--
(lamp shade)

I say--don't wear shades--
let all see your eyes shine.

Be open to the complete picture---
Here Now.
Seeing, Hearing and Sharing
In this Now Moment.

Grand Rising
by Cheryl

Dawn murmurs
through the tranquil mist--

Hush, and you will hear her golden melody.

Feel the luminous rays.

The sylphs are waking,
Hush--

murmurs become messages--
decipher the unintelligible--

Know the tranquil tone
of peace.

The original natural way
comes with every
Grand Rising--
Pulling the curtain
to another day.

"When The Angel's foot touches the Earth, the Earth trembles."
---*Christinemarie Spiritualdoorways*

the event
by Cheryl

I want to tell you about a gathering.

It is a Cosmic happening.

Some call it the Event.
It has been planned long in advance.

All are invited----
the ancients, the innocents---even those viewed
as guilty.

Our acceptance gives us admittance.
Our knowing is the ticket.
The practice of peace will be our map.

The Cosmic Rays show us the way,   a cipher,
they light up the path.

Sacred codes are hidden like Easter eggs.
We find them all over---
In nature, on our clocks and in our dreams.
We create them in music and art.

Our family are waiting for us---
they hail from far and near.
The sacred Earth clans are present---
tree, crystal, bird, wolf, bear and deer tribes,
AND
Those who have traveled a millennium to be present.
All are here---

The Divine Director pulls the curtain,
It is a beautiful scene,
Glorious light fills the room.

In the 5th Dimension
by Shianna Freeman

My consciousness flew to the 5th dimension, where the lotus blooms and the faeries play---
the outside being just as magikal as the inside.

It's a place where souls are unafraid
where LOVE is abundant and everyone is accepted.

We all understand each other, our infinite beauty is reflected.
We need no words to speak,
because it's all energetic innerstanding.

We dance and sing and play while the colors of our souls are blended.
Nothing here is slippery, we're all rooted and grounded.

True Love is Unconditional.
The circle of trust is perfectly round.

Love Unconditional
by Jennifer H.

The matrix has people
fooled to think
that love is weak

One of the ways
it keeps people asleep

People greatly underestimate

The strength it takes
to look at what

The world deems as ugly
take it in your heart
and let the judgment fall apart

The determination that is needed
to feel all the pain and let it go
drain down into the earth to be healed

The magic that is necessary
to face your fears with love
and transmute them

The energy it takes
to stand tall
through all the
shame, blame and guilt
they try to bury you with

The bravery it takes
to speak up and say
Enough is Enough
I'm done playing "this" game

I Love Myself
Love Unconditional

Gentle
by Cody Ray Richardson

Gentle
Gentle giant
Gentle
you don't have to fight it
Gentle
It's enough that your try'n
Gentle
You have come out of hid'in

Gentle
The flow knows you're com'in
Gentle
No use In run'in
Gentle
You must woe it in
Gentle
Acceptance hugs discipline

Gentle
The universe responds
Gentle
To those who are calm
Gentle
Excess N deficiency
Gentle
Open and you will see

Gentle
Contractions N expansions
Gentle
Tents to mansions
Gentle
Hold N let go
Gentle
Only you can know

Gentle
What it is you need
Gentle
In a world ever changing

Gentle
Sometimes not getting what you want
Gentle
Will lead you to your cause

Gentle
It's ok to lose
Gentle
The battle has been fought
Gentle
All is good and well
Gentle
Between heaven and hell

Gentle
Rest your broken heart
Gentle
Let it fall apart
Gentle
Let come back together again
Gentle
Change is your medicine

Gentle
I see the stars in your eyes
Gentle
All will make sense in time
Gentle
Then confusion will set in
Gentle
Gentle and you'll be lost again

The space will be open
Gentle
As wide as the ocean
Gentle
We all have to learn to swim
Gentle
Until we meet again

Be gentle

Just Be
by Cheryl

I'm back on the hamster wheel---

       gettin up early--
       put on my best clean clothes--
       pack a lunch--

Push along on the highway--
Watch out for potholes.

I'm on the road again---
this time--
I'm happy to help.
What can I do to assist you?
Just be there--
a listening ear,
at a safe place for others,
just stay safe too.

Rules and Boundaries--
learn them--enforce them--
Be them.
Or not!

Mastery
by Le'Vell Zimmerman

The Ego minds expectations are limited.

It's only necessary to ground yourself and
acknowledge that you wrote this story, where all
is taking place for your greatest benefit on all levels.

Great emotional maturity and openness is in letting go
of the minds endless questions and relaxing beloved.

Following your joy and trusting the process is the
disposition of Mastery.

The Ego Mind identities endless questions and
attempts to "figure things out" is often rooted in
fear in wanting to know how it all works,
when this is the nature of the path of self realization itself.

*You are literally showing yourself through this linear journey,
where attempting to "jump ahead of yourself" is where you miss
what you are attempting to show yourself through the process.*

As long as you are attempting to protect yourself
in anticipation of "the unknown", you are creating
chaos through holding on to the Ego Minds fear
and over analysis.

Love is beyond all logical comprehension.

Here is where you recognize the importance of inner stillness.

All is well indeed.

Many thanks to these contributors:

Bob Dunham

Maria Lodes

Darrel Johannes

Cody Ray Richardson

Omanassa Star

Mercy Talley

Susan Grace

Mary Long

Marcie Bakker

Gracia Penttinen

Le'Vell Zimmerman

Mitchell T. Miller

Alyssa Narum

Emily River

Eden Sky

A'Marie B. Thomas-Brown

Varunvir Punj

Christinemarie Spiritualdoorways

Shianna Freeman

Jennifer H.

and the anonymous poet

Author page--

Cheryl Lunar Wind lives in the Mount Shasta area in a little town called Weed. She is a practicer of Mayan cosmology, Lakota ceremony, Star Knowledge and the Universal Laws including the Law of One. Her hobbies are writing poetry, music, dance, drum circles and love for all life; plant, animal and crystal. Cheryl has been a guide and spiritual teacher for many years. Now she shares wisdom and wit through poetry, and has published poetry books; Know Your Way, We Are One, Follow the White Rabbit, Love Your Light, LIFE: Shared thru Poetry, Come to Mount Shasta: Sacred Path Poetry, We Are Light, Finding Our Way Home, We Are Forever, Handshake With the Divine and now Grand Rising: A New Day Has Dawned.

Testimonials---

"Cheryl's poetry is very inspiring--particularly the way she compares life with the forces of nature. There is a special element in her poems that opens my heart and fills my soul with divine possibilities."
Giovanna Taormina, Co-Founder, One Circle Foundation

"Cheryl's poems have helped me to uncover and honor my own hidden memories. The beauty of her spirit is evident in each tender, insightful passage."
Marguerite Lorimer, www.earthalive.com

"A rare collection filled with raw, courageous honesty. Thought provoking words that will stop you in your tracks."
Snow Thorner, ED Open Sky Gallery, Montague, California

"When wisdom, guidance, confirming comfort, ect. arrives to us humans--from beings with the perspective of other realms--it is a divine gift. Especially in the form of what we call poetry, and through a being with no agenda; Cheryl Lunar Wind simply shares what source gives her!"
--Dragon Love (Thomas) Budde

Cheryl,
Greetings and Happy Monday to you my friend. I just wanted to share with you that every time I read 'Come to Mount Shasta', even now that I'm mentioning it I cry, I cannot help it, it is such a Divine message and so impeccable in its timing. I came up here for Spirit, you know I was called by Source and I live on the mountain and I just want to thank you. Your poem found me last summer at the headwaters during the Alien and Angels conference; and then I found your book sitting in the gazebo and I just can't stop, I love it! I love you, thank you.
---Jim

Cheryl,
Just want to thank you for your bringing me into the community at Shasta. What you are doing/did do is absolutely changing my life. You did it, you were instrumental in helping me set my true path. Spirit is moving and the more of us that listen and act the sooner the shift will be completed.
---Darrel

About Cheryl's poetry--
"You are dynamic! I have known no one who does so much so swiftly, and your writing touches my heart because it comes from your heart."
---The Durwood Show

"Your words are my words. I keep your book 'Know Your Way' on my nightstand. I read it at bedtime and morning."
---Karina Arroyo

"Cheryl's words work magic in my heart, stirring the wisdom that is buried so deeply within me---beautiful indeed!"
---Ellie Pfeiffer, founder of Ellie's Espresso & Bakery, Weed, CA

www.ingramcontent.com/pod-product-compliance
Lightning Source LLC
Chambersburg PA
CBHW061259040426
42444CB00010B/2430